ONE EUROPE

Nancy Dunnan

THE MILLBROOK PRESS

Brookfield, Connecticut

Published by The Millbrook Press
2 Old New Milford Road
Brookfield, CT 06804
© 1992 Blackbirch Graphics, Inc.
First Edition

Created and produced in association with Blackbirch Graphics.
Series Editor: Bruce S. Glassman

Library of Congress Cataloging-in-Publication Data
Dunnan, Nancy.
    One Europe / Nancy Dunnan.
    Includes bibliographical references and index.
    Summary: Discusses the impact, both internal and external, of the
regulations that will govern the member countries of the European
Economic Community beginning in 1992.
    1. European Economic Community—Juvenile literature. 2. Europe
1992—Juvenile literature. [1. European Economic Community.
2. Europe 1992.] I. Title. II. Series.
ISBN 1-878841-96-3 (pbk)
HC241.2.D86   1992
337.1. '42—dc20
                                                    91-30083
                                                         CIP
                                                          AC

Contents

Chapter **1**

The Idea of a European Community

The year is set: 1992. Plans that have taken decades to develop will be set in motion. Twelve European nations—Belgium, Denmark, France, Germany, Greece, Ireland, Italy, Luxembourg, the Netherlands, Portugal, Spain, and the United Kingdom—will merge into one integrated economic community. But what exactly will this new community entail? What will it mean to the citizens of each of these twelve countries? And what will this union mean to the rest of the world?

Right now, the answers to those questions must remain somewhat incomplete. Although the major governing rules of the European Community have been worked out, and proposed plans for economic stimulation and reorganization have been announced, no one knows just how all the elements of the new community are going to function in the "real world." Only time will tell that.

Even with all the unknowns, one thing remains clear: The creation of a united European Community is a daring and complex undertaking. Success depends upon the complete cooperation of twelve very different countries, each with a highly defined sense of identity and a fierce sense of national pride. In becoming an EC member nation, each country sacrifices some of its autonomy and independence for a greater good.

The creation of a united Europe is a daring and complex task

Opposite:
The EC flag waves above the flags of the member nations in Rome during a Community summit.

THE EUROPEAN COMMUNITY

NORTHERN IRELAND

IRELAND

GREAT BRITAIN

BELGIUM

FRANCE

ATLANTIC OCEAN

PORTUGAL

SPAIN

MEDITERRANEAN

Member country

Non-member country

0   500 mi.

0   500 km.

MOROCCO   ALGERIA

Many Europeans—though in favor of joining the Community—are wary of just what their country will be sacrificing in terms of culture and identity. Until the tangible benefits of economic union are felt in the pocketbooks of the citizens, enthusiasm for the EC plan will be tempered by a healthy skepticism. Citizens are also concerned by a

number of other matters that will affect their daily lives but are, as yet, not fully worked out. Debates and questions about the proposed use of a common EC currency, the construction of a central bank, and the use of a "Community language" today form the basis of many discussions throughout the twelve member nations.

Regardless of how future plans work out, what has been achieved so far is truly remarkable. And even though the process of unification has been fraught with conflict and discord, world leaders from twelve powerful nations have been able to hammer out a means by which each country can function happily as part of a larger structure. Their efforts so far are a tribute to the universal values of cooperation and compromise; they stand as an impressive example for other nations around the world. Still, the ultimate success of this brand new union will take years, even decades, to actually be seen.

Unity by Choice

The goal of one Europe might seem easy, especially to those who live in places like the United States or Canada, where people travel freely from state to state or province to province. Yet it's not so easy for Europeans. They have many ancient barriers, the most obvious and critical one being the physical frontiers or borders of each country.

The United States was divided by a border once, during the Civil War, when the North and South were enemies. But our history is short compared to the countries of Europe. There, for thousands of years, various countries were fierce enemies. War has ravaged Europe, changing its landscape and instilling mistrust among its people.

What we know today as Germany, for example, has not always been that way. Its territory has expanded and contracted as the result of many conflicts. World War II caused the most damage, eventually slicing the country in two: East and West Germany. Although today Germany is again one, you can still see the ruins of the war in Berlin, the city that was literally divided in half. So, too, can you see ruins throughout Europe. In Italy, for example, there are many buildings and churches left from the days when the Roman Empire controlled much of the world.

Over the centuries, empire builders, from Caesar to Charlemagne to Napoleon, have tried to impose unity on

French Emperor Napoleon Bonaparte had dreams of uniting Europe under his reign. By 1812, his empire included France, Holland, Belgium, and Luxembourg, with control over western Germany, Poland, Spain, and most of Italy.

Europe. Philosophers and people of various political persuasions, too, have discussed the idea of a unified Europe for hundreds of years. Yet nationalism often prevailed and nations have more often than not remained solely involved in their own problems, with little time for those of their neighbors.

Everyone—dictators, kings, emperors—wanted a piece of the pie. And for many years there were *empires*, rather than separate states. With so many years of hatred and bloodshed behind these countries, it is particularly notable that Europe's present economic unity is, for once, not an imposed one, but one based on *choice*. The EC has used democratic decision-making processes and a series of peaceful treaties to improve the basic standard of living for all of Europe's people.

Unity by Force

Much of Europe has been "unified" in the past. But unification was always by the force of aggressive conquerors and emperors.

• **The Roman Empire**, at its height in A.D. 117, included Great Britain, France, Belgium, the Netherlands, Luxembourg, Liechtenstein, Italy, Spain, Portugal, Germany, Switzerland, Austria, Hungary, Romania, Greece, Bulgaria, Albania, Yugoslavia, Turkey, and the part of Russia between the Black and Caspian Seas, as well as northern Africa and western Asia.

• **The Frankish Empire**, under Clovis, flourished from A.D. 486 to 507 and included France, Belgium, the Netherlands, Luxembourg, and much of western Germany.

• **The Byzantine Empire**, the eastern remnants of the Roman Empire, extended into Europe by the end of Clovis's reign. In the 500s, it included the southern and eastern shores of the Mediterranean, the Balkans, Turkey, and coastal parts of France and Italy.

• **Charlemagne's Empire,** which followed that of Clovis, extended the Frankish Empire. Charlemagne was named the first Holy Roman Emperor by the Pope. He extended the boundaries to include the areas of Europe from southern France to Denmark and from Italy to what are now the borders of the Soviet Union. Charlemagne's era lasted from A.D. 768 to 814.

• **The Holy Roman Empire**, was run by German kings for almost nine hundred years—from A.D. 962 to 1806. Slightly smaller than Charlemagne's Empire, it retained most of Europe from eastern France and northern Italy through the western parts of Austria, Czechoslovakia, and Poland.

• **The Turkish-based Ottoman Empire**, at its height in 1566, controlled most of Africa, plus the Balkan peninsula and parts of Austria and Hungary.

• **The Empire of Napoleon**, was built by the man who crowned himself emperor of France. In 1812, his French Empire included France, Holland, Belgium, and Luxembourg, and he controlled western Germany, Poland, Spain, and most of Italy. After Napoleon's defeat, Europe was content with smaller empires—the Austro-Hungarian and the Prussian, to name two.

• **World War II's Axis Empire**, the last attempt to unify Europe, was headed by Germany's Adolf Hitler and Italy's Benito Mussolini. At the peak of its force, in September 1942, it included all the countries of Europe between Russia and the English Channel except for Spain, Portugal, Sweden, Switzerland, and Finland.

The Axis Empire, like the many that came before it, failed because it was an unnatural unity based on aggression and domination. Although military might and oppressive rule can hold an empire together for many years, a permanent unity can only be based on cooperation and mutual need.

Nazis march through Germany, during a rally on September 7, 1938.

The European Council met in October 1990 to discuss economic and monetary union. In the left foreground is Italian Premier Giulio Andreotti.

How It Began

The idea of a united Europe might never have arisen had it not been for the devastation left by World War II. After the war, economic unity became a more appealing concept: Western Europe was no longer a significant power; France and England subsequently lost most of their colonies in Africa and Asia; and Germany was divided in two. In the meantime, the Soviet Union and the United States quickly emerged as the world's leading powers, and much of Western Europe became economically and militarily dependent on the United States.

The Council of Europe

Based on their shared traditions as well as the need to promote economic well-being in the aftermath of World War II, ten European countries set up the Council of Europe in 1949. The Council did not focus on national defense or military activities, but instead promoted closer unity among its members in order to bring about both economic and social progress. As time went on, more countries joined the council. Today there are twenty-three members. This organization was the first attempt by a number of European states to join forces in an effort to help one another protect the political and cultural heritage of all of Europe.

The Treaty of Paris

During the post-World War II period, one person in particular made a great impact in the trend toward a united Europe: Jean Monnet. In 1950, this French statesman promoted the idea of unification based on common economic needs. He approached France's foreign minister, Robert Schuman, with an idea. He suggested the pooling of French and German coal and steel resources. Schuman liked Monnet's idea and had him draft a document known as the Schuman Declaration. This declaration said that "the gathering of the nations of Europe requires the elimination of the age-old opposition of France and Germany."

French Foreign Minister Robert Schuman oversaw the signing and implementation of the Treaty of Paris in 1951.

Jean Monnet was the first statesman to promote the idea of economic unification within Europe. Here, Monnet delivers an inaugural speech outling the responsiblities of the ECSC, which was established by the Treaty of Paris.

The declaration put Franco-German coal and steel production under a common authority. The long-term objective of the Schuman Declaration was to unite Europe by joining forces economically, beginning with steel and coal.

A year later, in 1951, Belgium, France, Italy, Luxembourg, the Netherlands, and West Germany signed the Treaty of Paris. This treaty established the European Coal and Steel Community, or ECSC. Sometimes the Treaty of Paris is called the Schuman Plan in honor of the French foreign minister who oversaw its implementation.

By 1953, the ECSC had established a common market among its six member nations for the production of coal, steel, iron ore, and scrap metal by removing trade barriers among all the members. It also allowed coal and steel

Jean Monnet

Jean Monnet in 1979

Often called the "architect of the EC," Jean Monnet, was born in Cognac, France, in 1888. Monnet directed Allied supply operations during World War I, getting war materials, food, and other supplies for the Allies. Then, from 1919 to 1923, Monnet served as deputy secretary general of the League of Nations. During these post-war years he was instrumental in helping to stabilize the economies of several countries, including Austria, Algeria, Poland, and Romania.

During World War II, Monnet was a financial adviser to Britain and the United States, serving as a member of the Washington-based British Supply Council. Following the war, he devised the Monnet Plan, a five-year program for France's economic recovery. He outlined ways for France to modernize its industries and agriculture.

In the 1950s and 1960s, Monnet led the movement to unify Western Europe. More than any other single person, he was responsible for the sequence of events that led to the creation of the European Community. It was he who initially suggested to Robert Schuman the idea of a European Coal and Steel Community. The Schuman Plan established the European Coal and Steel Community, of which Monnet was the first president. He served as president from 1952 to 1955.

In 1955, Monnet left the European Coal and Steel Community to form the Action Committee for the United States of Europe, also instrumental in helping unite Europe economically. He became that group's first chairman as well. He died in France, in 1979.

workers from any member country to work in any other member country. Perhaps even more significant was the fact that the ECSC established an important precedent: It required member nations to surrender some of their autonomy to the ECSC, which would then make certain rules that all member nations would follow. This cooperative spirit was a major breakthrough on the path toward a united Europe.

The Treaties of Rome

Based on its success, the ECSC and its six members agreed to broaden their cooperation by signing the two Treaties of Rome in 1957. One of these treaties established the European Economic Community (EEC). This group set about removing barriers that made moving goods, workers, and capital (money and investments) among its member nations extremely expensive and time consuming. The other treaty established the European Atomic Energy

Community (Euratom) to work together to develop nuclear energy for peaceful purposes. Both the EEC and Euratom went into effect in 1958. The ECSC, Euratom, and EEC eventually merged into one administrative system that is generally called the European Community.

Great Britain, Denmark, and Ireland joined the EC in 1973. Greece joined in 1981, and Portugal and Spain joined in 1986. Then in 1990, when East Germany and West Germany merged as a united Germany, East Germans were added to the Community.

Steps Forward and Backward

During the 1960s and 1970s, cooperation among the members did not move forward as smoothly as had been hoped. It was hard for member nations to put the needs of the European Community above the needs of their individual countries. In fact, if one country felt that a proposed ruling would threaten the economic well being of one of its own home industries, it was almost sure to veto that ruling.

Statesmen from the six countries of the ECSC sign the Treaties of Rome in 1957. West Germany's Chancellor and Foreign Minister Konrad Adenauer (center) signs as the other ministers prepare to do the same.

Paul Henri Spaak of Belgium (right) and Joseph Bech of Luxembourg sit behind a pile of documents that make up the text of the Common Market Membership Treaty. Upon signing this treaty in 1973, Great Britain, Denmark, and Ireland became official members of the European Community.

Various economic setbacks in the 1970s—a recession and sharp increases in the cost of oil—caused countries to worry more about protecting themselves than about the well-being of their fellow Europeans. Some countries imposed border taxes and re-established trade quotas in order to protect the jobs of their own workers. In doing so, they undid some of the progress that had been made toward unification.

Despite the fact that the Treaties of Rome, which established the EEC, had set clear goals for doing away with all tariffs and quotas among member nations, it didn't happen. It would, in fact, take many more years to actually accomplish. During this period of setbacks and disillusionment, some people actually referred to the unification of Europe as "Eurosclerosis," a play on the word "arteriosclerosis" (hardening of the arteries in the human body).

The Single European Act

A renewed drive to unite Europe came about in the 1980s as many countries recovered from recessions and benefited from substantial economic growth. Unity was also spurred on in 1985 by the Single European Act (SEA), in which far-reaching reforms of the original treaties were made. SEA set up ways to continue the work that had been started. It also incorporated about three hundred proposals that would eliminate barriers to a unified market by the end of 1992. Some of the proposals will be discussed in greater detail throughout the following chapters.

The first meeting of the nine-nation Common Market was held in Paris in 1973.

Chapter 2

The World Within a United Europe

Why a united Europe? What prompted these countries to begin a process of unification? And what are the advantages of a European Community? A united Europe will make it easier, less costly, and less time consuming to do business and to travel among the member nations. It will also make the member nations and their products and services more competitive with those of other major industrial countries, especially the United States and Japan.

Imagine, for a minute, that North and South Carolina are two different countries. The people on each side of the state line speak different languages, eat different foods, have different lifestyles, use different money, and have different laws.

You live in North Carolina; your mother's family, however, lives in South Carolina. Even though the distance between Charlotte, N.C., (where you live) and Charleston, S.C., (where they live) is only 177 miles, you have to adapt to a whole different world when you visit your grandmother. You must plan your trip in advance and exchange your North Carolina money into South Carolina currency at the available rates. And you must carry your passport and customs declaration forms with you so they can be checked at the border.

> Each of the member nations has made compromises to be part of a larger whole

Opposite:
An official flag-raising ceremony at the EEC Palace in Belgium.

EC CHANGES AT A GLANCE

After 1992, EC nations wil be changed in the following ways:

- Countries will be united as one economic unit, with a market of 340 million people.

- Tariffs between countries will be removed.

- "Borders" will be eliminated, allowing free travel between member nations and freer flow of goods and money throughout the EC.

- Four-branch system of government will be in place for daily operation of EC business.

These laws apply not only to you and other people, but also to any goods and products being taken across the border. For example, all clothes, food, and furniture arriving at the border must be checked and approved before they can be moved into another country. Each shipment or item must be accompanied by official papers, and very often tariffs or taxes must be paid. All of this takes time and is expensive. If your grandmother wants to send you a desk or computer for your birthday, it may take weeks or months to reach you because of all the red tape involved in sending it from North Carolina to South Carolina.

Now substitute Spain and Portugal for North and South Carolina. Or England and Ireland. Or Belgium and France. For many years, the countries we collectively refer to as "Europe" have been living and conducting business just as in the example. Goods were stopped at every country's borders (sometimes called "frontiers") for approval and to collect various taxes. That meant truck drivers carrying furniture from Denmark to Spain had to stop at every border along the way to fill out many complicated customs papers.

Checking goods did not apply just to big-ticket items like cars. For years, German law prohibited the sale of beer brewed in other countries because the additives they contain went against German "purity laws." And Italian law used to prohibit the marketing of pasta not made from duram, a specific type of wheat.

Travelers were also stopped for immigration checks, to make certain that their passports or ID cards were up to date and valid. Customs officials also collected duty (money) on certain goods that travelers had purchased. Luggage was examined for security purposes—to see, for instance, if there were illegal items inside.

In this process of crossing borders, travelers and those shipping and carrying goods had to fill out many forms. Some forms simply collected facts and statistics for the country's government. Other forms were designed to control plant and animal diseases, or to stop restricted exports and imports, to enforce trade quotas, and to keep out banned products.

So you can see that such regulations added many extra costs to doing business between countries. In fact, the rules often discouraged such business.

The Role of Competition

Competition is another reason why these twelve countries are coming together. In order to compete with other (bigger) nations in today's global marketplace, European countries have had to join forces. There's simply no way Portugal, for example, with approximately 10 million inhabitants, can compete with Japan's 130 million people. Yet when Portugal merges with its neighbors, it is a part of a force to be reckoned with.

The twelve countries in the European Community represent 340 million people—potentially the largest single market for goods and services in the world. By way of comparison, the United States market is 245 million consumers. This one European market is expected to produce

$4.5 trillion in goods and services each year, putting it right behind the United States and ahead of Japan.

So, despite the problems, the European Community is hoping to accomplish something that Americans take for granted: the free movement of people, goods, services, and capital across state lines. It is also aiming to improve the working conditions and salaries of its citizens. One key way the EC is bringing about this change is by removing internal tariffs—those taxes previously described—between member nations. Why, you may wonder, do the Europeans want to do this—give up the revenue they have been collecting in tariffs from one another? The answer is quite simple: Without tariff barriers, quotas, and other restrictions between these countries, there will be more jobs and more products and services available, and prices will be significantly lower.

Once united, the twelve nations of the EC will create a powerful production bloc that will exceed that of Japan or the United States. This will make the EC a highly competitive force in the world market. Here, a German technician works in a German Ford auto factory.

The Seeds of Change

The economic unification of the twelve EC nations has been in progress for a long time—since the end of World War II, when a devastated Europe sought ways to rebuild its economy and prevent future holocausts. The move toward unification was helped along by better communication and transportation, both of which brought the peoples of Europe and their leaders closer together. At this time, several organizations were established to work on issues of common concern. Energy and free trade were the two most important issues. The organizations eventually joined forces and established the European Community, or EC. Part of the reason it has taken so long, and part of the reason why all the details are still not finalized (and probably won't be until at least 1994), is that the countries involved are so diverse. Their many complex laws and entrenched customs make compromise for the good of "one Europe" extremely difficult.

The Benefits

Europe's economic unification will, over time, bring about a better business environment. Not only will products become cheaper due to the elimination of import and export fees, there will be more jobs and more opportunities for workers and students. A British doctor will be able to practice medicine in Spain; a Greek student may study in Italy. Europeans will have more spending power, lifestyles will improve, and people will have more choices.

Remember the desk your grandmother was going to send you? In Europe before 1992, it would be subject to an array of import and export taxes. It would have to go through customs inspections and would take a long time to reach you. But with the elimination of borders, all products (including food and raw material) will be cheaper. The taxes and the huge pile of paperwork will be eliminated. There will only be one form. In fact, it already exists: the Single Administrative Document, a straightforward questionnaire.

At the same time, unification will ease the way for setting up larger corporations, which, in turn, will be more competitive within world markets. Already, European businesses are moving to take advantage of the open market. Small- to medium-sized companies that have been profitable under protectionist rules in their own countries are buying firms in other EC member states in order to survive after 1992. These "acquisitions," once thought of as a hallmark of American big business, are taking place throughout Europe.

Experts forecast that the single market could very well result in five percent overall growth in the near future, as well as a marked slowdown in the rate of inflation and a further decline in the number of people out of work. They

Economic unification is expected to make products cheaper while it stimulates business throughout the member nations. These changes should create better job opportunities for workers and improve the lifestyles of all the EC's citizens.

Developing stronger agricultural markets and technology is one of the primary objectives of the EC.

also expect that between two million and five million new jobs will be created. We will talk more about specific economic benefits in Chapter 4.

Unresolved Problems

It's not surprising that there are difficulties and squabbles among the EC nations. To understand these disagreements, think for a minute about America's thirteen original colonies. The people spoke the same language and shared similar customs, lifestyles, and goals. In contrast, the twelve EC countries are much more diverse. They have longstanding cultural differences and are all already sovereign states, several of them with *hundreds* of years of independence behind them. They all have distinct politics, separate administrative and legal systems, and widely

What Is the ECU?

Look up the word *ecu* in most big dictionaries and you'll find two entries, both derived from the French. The first is "a shield carried by knights in the Middle Ages"; the second, "any of several gold and silver coins of France from the fourteenth century onward." Today, ECU is the abbreviation for the European Currency Unit, the currency unit of the European Monetary System, which was introduced on January 1, 1979. It was put into effect through an agreement between the central banks of the member states.

Think of the ECU as a grab-bag or basket comprising differing proportions of each national currency. All of the currencies of the Community except Portugal's escudo and Greece's drachma participate in the exchange rate mechanism (they will become part of the system as soon as their economies are stronger). Amounts are determined in accordance with the economic size of the member countries, and are revised every five years. The value of the ECU is determined by using the current

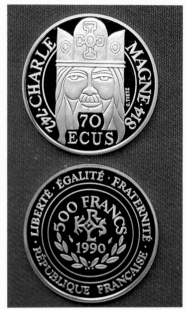

A French version of the ECU

market rate of each member nation's currency.

The European Monetary System operates on the principle of stable, but flexible exchange rates. The ECU isn't legal tender yet— there are no bills or coins to speak of—but financial markets are convinced that it will be. They believe that one day, all EC citizens will

trade in their pounds, marks, and francs for ECUs. And, in fact, a majority of EC residents are in favor of a single currency. In 1990, the Paris-based Association for the Monetary Union of Europe polled six thousand adults in all twelve EC countries and found that sixty-one percent favored the replacement of their currencies by the ECU within six years. Seventy-six percent approved the creation of a European central bank. Pro-ECU sentiment was strongest in France (seventy-three percent) and weakest in Britain (thirty-seven percent). Germany was divided, fifty-one percent in favor, forty-nine percent opposed.

Much remains to be decided, and EC leaders still have to thrash out details about monetary union. It is likely the world won't see the ECU used until 1994.

So far, the ECU has been established as the Community's accounting unit. It has also become popular for private financial instruments such as bonds. The ECU ranks among the top five currencies in international bond issues.

differing historical experiences. Now you can understand why they have some difficulty agreeing!

And so, even though 1992 is the official year of unification, not every EC proposal is ready to be implemented by the end of the year. The success of some proposals that have already become law will remain a question mark for some time to come. In realistic terms, we can't expect to see the real results of *everything* until 1994. Some predict we won't see certain changes until the year 2000.

The five key problems that remain unsolved revolve around money (Should there or shouldn't there be a universal currency?); around banking (How can *one central bank* serve all of Europe?); around immigration (Who should be let in? What sort of restrictions apply?); around trading laws (What kind of rules will best help the EC compete globally?); and around defense (What sort of military does the EC need?). Let's look at each of these unresolved questions.

Money Problems

Today, each country has its own currency and each currency has a different value. These currencies fluctuate in value according to economic trends within that country and with its trading partners. Thus, much of the process of doing business internationally requires keeping track of the different rates of exchange from one currency to the next.

As an example, say you want to convert British pounds to Italian lira. To get the most for your money, you'll want to check what the exchange rate is. As we said, it fluctuates depending on the international supply and demand for various currencies. So one day, you might be able to get 1,200 lira for a pound, the next day 1,400.

To help solve the problem of the ever-changing rates, the EC has established a common rate of exchange based on the European Currency Unit, or ECU. This unit defines the official value of each member's currency. Each country's currency has an official price in ECUs and therefore is linked to every other member country's money. In the most simplistic terms, the EC wants the ECU to be to the European economy what the dollar is to the United States economy.

So far, however, it's not working. And, in fact, this is one of the hottest issues the EC is tackling. Many countries have reservations about the ECU's overall benefits. The most outspoken opponents, notably former British Prime Minister Margaret Thatcher and Germany's former

A coin minted with a symbol of the united Europe shows a woman with the flags of the member nations flowing in her hair.

central bank president, Karl Otto Pohl, point out that EC members have widely varying inflation rates (rates at which prices rise). Greece, Spain, and Portugal also have doubts. Their main fear is that once a single currency is created, they would lose the power to lower the value of their own money, a successful—and quite often used—tool for boosting exports.

Right now, the ECU is used only as a benchmark against which to measure all other currencies. It is not a currency you would find, for example, if you went on vacation to Greece tomorrow. Governments have not yet made it legal tender; there is no European Central Bank responsible for the ECU, and no ECU bank notes or coins have been issued. (The minting of ECU coins in some EC countries, including Belgium, France, and Spain, is primarily a symbolic gesture intended to give support to their determination to eventually achieve an economic and monetary union in Europe.)

When the single currency is issued (and, of course, the big issue remains *when*—some predict 1994 and others say definitely not until the year 2000) it will most likely be similar to the dollar, with denominations in one, five, ten, twenty, and fifty unit notes. There will most likely also be one, five, ten, and twenty-five unit coins.

What will the currency look like? Again, there are may ideas. Bertrand De Maigret of the Association of Monetary Union says school children will compete to design the currency, which is likely to differ from country to country, with just one side identical in every member country. In this way, for example, the British could continue to have their queen on one side. Others suggest that famous Europeans of the past, like Dutch philosopher Erasmus, should be on the bills, while others point to Jean Monnet, the French founder of the EC, as the most logical and least controversial candidate.

The European Flag

The European flag looks quite similar to the flag of America's thirteen original colonies. That flag, called the Grand Union flag, had a circle of thirteen white stars on a field of blue. The EC flag has twelve stars, in a circle, against a blue sky. The twelve golden stars represent the lasting union of the twelve member nations. The points of the stars do not touch each other and their circle is in the exact middle of the flag. All the stars have five points; the top point of each star in the circle points straight up.

The flag itself is a rectangle, of which the breadth is one and a half times the height.

Politically, the debate over a common currency has divided the member nations. Germany has pushed to tie the use of a common currency to greater monetary and political union among the members. In November, 1991, Britain's John Major said that tying a common currency to greater political union was unacceptable. Although Major agreed to a European currency by the year 2000, an aide said Britain would likely veto any treaty that expands the decision-making powers of the Commission or the European Parliament.

The ECU *is* being used by the EC's financial markets as a means of trading. There are ECU traveler's checks, bank deposits, and bank loans. It is also used by some businesses as a currency for invoicing and payment. ECU bonds have also been sold on international markets—the first ECU bonds were sold in the United States in 1984. The ECU's most important function is as a currency for loans and transactions between banks. On the international bond market it is one of the top five currencies.

A Central Bank

Another topic of discord between nations has been whether or not to establish a central bank. Again, many countries have been against it: They each have their own way of handling money and doing business and are not yet in agreement over how to compromise for the good of one. Imagine *your* neighbor telling you what to do with your savings account. Indeed, it is quite unlikely that the central bank of Germany (the Bundesbank), for example, which has its own monetary policies and rules, will allow the Central Bank of Italy or the Bank of England to tell it how to manage German currency. Nor does it want a central EC bank to run its affairs.

The institution, if established, will be called the European Central Bank. There *is* consensus in principle regarding the bank's general features. Essentially, it will be modeled on the German Bundesbank and the Federal

Leaders from the member nations met in London in 1991 to move forward on plans for developing a central bank.

Reserve Bank in the United States. Both are known throughout the world for their efforts in keeping inflation rates low in their countries.

The central bank will be responsible for the monetary policies of the member states. In the beginning, it will primarily coordinate the activities of each individual country's central bank. Eventually, however, it would be responsible for administering the Community's single currency and would be responsible for the exchange rate. In addition, the bank would be committed to price stability and would be independent from national and EC governments. It would be accountable only to the democratic institutions, namely the Parliament. The bank would develop and implement the common monetary policies; take part in national banking supervision and international monetary cooperation; and provide loans to poorer regions.

The EC is still debating the questions of protectionism and open competition with other countries. Many member countries argue that, if trade barriers are lowered to American and Japanese manufacturers, European nations will be forced to develop more competitive products. Some say this competition will be good for the EC; others say it will put a strain on most European manufacturing.

Protectionism

In the past, governments often subsidized or supported certain key industries or companies within their country. These subsidies consisted of actual cash payments or exemptions from paying certain taxes. These arrangements "protected" select companies or industries. Now, the EC wants to do away with such protectionism, so that all companies will compete on an equal scale.

So, what will happen to a British insurance company when British customers can purchase cheaper insurance from the French? Will the Germans be happy when their key industries relocate to another country where labor is cheaper? How will Irish bankers feel when Irish people put their savings in Belgian banks? These real-life situations will probably lead to the "survival of the fittest."

It's not surprising, then, that some companies are afraid of competition. They fear, perhaps realistically so, that they may fail once they are subject to open competition. Aside from just competing with Italy or Belgium, for example, British companies will have to compete more readily with Japan and the United States. Some companies undoubtedly will fail, and people will lose their jobs. By some estimates, as many as half of all the companies in the EC may fail once they are subject to open competition. If this is true, hundreds of thousands of people will lose their jobs. On the other hand, with more competition, people will be able to get better quality goods and lower prices. This will stimulate the economy and create more work.

Fortress Europe

Just how competitive the EC will become in world markets will not be seen until after 1992. If the EC lowers trade barriers to American and Japanese products—automobiles and electronic equipment in particular—then the European nations will be forced to develop more competitive products. On the other hand, the EC could decide to form a closed trading bloc, keeping out products from non-European countries. If that happens, and it seems unlikely that it will, competition will suffer because most European products will only be sold within the member nations. They won't have to compete in world markets and quality will go down as prices go up. Other nations would take the opportunity to place high duties on European goods.

Experts call the possibility of the EC erecting new barriers around its external borders "Fortress Europe." The term is really a misnomer. It is meant to mean that internal markets would open up while external markets would close down. Officials of the EC repeatedly emphasize that they are not building a new "Europe for Europe," they are building a new Europe for the global economy. The EC Commission recently issued a statement in response to this concern. The statement said that "1992 Fortress Europe will not be a fortress Europe but a partnership Europe."

In fact, the hope is that new trade agreements under the auspices of the General Agreement on Tariffs and Trade (GATT) will reduce barriers to world trade and will lessen the risk of "trade wars" in which countries raise ever higher barriers. Such trade wars helped lead to the Great Depression of the 1930s.

Although there is talk of "Fortress Europe," there is also talk of "Fortress America." In 1990, the United States and Canada agreed to remove trade barriers between the two countries over the next ten years. Such bilateral agreements will help the United States better compete with the new Europe.

Expanded Trading Bloc

On October 22, 1991, the twelve-nation European Community and the seven-member European Free Trade Association (EFTA) wrapped up two years of tough negotiations centering on building a gigantic trading bloc. (The EFTA nations are Sweden, Austria, Switzerland, Norway, Finland, Iceland, and Liechtenstein.) The two groups agreed to form a new common market known as the European Economic Area. The agreement allows for goods, services, and money to move freely among the nineteen member nations and is scheduled to begin as soon as January 1, 1993.

It is expected that the new European Economic Area trade bloc will mean tougher global competition for the United States and Japan, especially in agriculture, textiles, and automobiles. The trade alliance will embrace more

THE COUNTRIES OF THE NEW TRADING BLOC

- European Community
- Free-Trade Association Member

than 380 million Western European consumers from the Arctic Circle to the Mediterranean Sea.

The agreement is subject to approval by each of the nineteen national parliaments. It appears, however, that most of the nations are eager to participate in the European Economic Area.

During the fall of 1991, the EC also stepped up negotiations with the United States for a trade accord. By November of that year Jacques Delors, president of the EC, said, "For the first time I am reasonably optimistic about the possibility of reaching an agreement."

Individual Country Goals

The freer movement of capital (money and investments being exchanged easily throughout the EC nations) allowed under the 1992 plan may also get in the way of the individual nations' ability to conduct independent financial policy. If, for example, France wants to increase taxes on business, it would be easy for French companies to simply move to a lower-tax country. Again, like the situations described already, these are only possibilities; they might happen, or they might not.

Immigration

What will happen when the EC borders are more open? Will there be a common immigration policy? The EC nations are aware that unrestricted immigration, especially

EC nations are fearful that unrestricted immigration policies would cause a disastrous influx of people from Eastern European countries and the Soviet Union.

from the economically weak countries of Eastern Europe and the Soviet Union, could be disastrous in terms of job competition and social welfare. A recent influx of East Germans into West Germany has already created a strain on the German economy, which may not be able to provide enough jobs or housing for its own citizens. Albanians are pouring into Italy, creating serious overcrowding problems there as well.

In recent years, the EC has absorbed some ten million legal immigrants—about half from North Africa—not to mention the tides of *illegal* ones that total at least several million. Compare this to the days when the United States was an immigrant nation and people poured through Ellis Island. Even today we have an immigration problem: people illegally crossing the border from Mexico to California and Texas; from Cuba to Florida; from the Dominican Republic to New York. The situation is much the same in Europe. In addition, there is the danger of a national backlash. In Italy, attacks against African and Arab immigrants have become commonplace. And in Berlin, ethnic violence has broken out between Germans and Turkish immigrants. Resentment is also rising against 900,000 Poles who entered Germany in 1990. Residents feel these immigrants add to existing social problems, including poverty, unemployment, homelessness, and crime. Many feel such a large new group puts too much stress on the existing systems of law enforcement, transportation, and social welfare programs.

The situation has started a scramble by the EC to shape, for the first time, a Communitywide policy on immigration. Up to now, France and Britain have opposed a common policy because they have tried to maintain special ties with former African and Asian colonies. What seems likely to emerge is a quota system for the entire EC similar to that of the United States, which sets annual levels and categories for immigrants. Once let in, the immigrants could circulate freely within the EC.

After 1992, the borders between EC member nations will essentially be erased.

So far, an immigration bill giving citizens the right to a five-year renewable passport has been bogged down, with no clear policy in sight as yet. Meanwhile, the EC is prodding the buffer states of Hungary, Czechoslovakia, and Poland to tighten up their borders with the Soviet Union to avoid further problems.

An All-European Army

Although France and Germany stood opposite each other in both World Wars I and II, they now want to become comrades in arms. Their two leaders—President François Mitterrand of France and Chancellor Helmut Kohl of Germany—have proposed a plan to build a joint European military force of 35,000 troops. The proposal, aimed at defending European unity, would expand the existing 5,000-troop Franco-German brigade by requiring nine European countries to contribute troops to the all-European security system.

Great Britain and Italy are against the plan because it rivals the North Atlantic Treaty Organization (NATO), which was formed after World War II and includes the United States and Canada. Douglas Hurd, Britain's foreign secretary, said it would be "useless and dangerous to overlap what NATO is doing." Instead, Britain and Italy want to work with NATO, not outside it. Other EC countries are also worried that the plan would lead to the withdrawal of U.S. troops from Europe.

But France and Germany say that if Europe is to become a true superpower it must free itself from depending on U.S. military forces. Such an all-European military force would indeed shift the balance of power away from the U.S. and toward the EC.

Social Issues

How businesses will operate in this changing economy is not the only concern once borders are lifted. What about laws regarding criminals? In the past, Europe has had a problem with terrorists and drug traffickers crossing into other countries without being properly checked. Will this problem get worse once customs checks are abolished? And what about socialized (government-controlled) medicine? A lot of decisions—some quite painful—will have to be made, and compromises will need to be met. Like anything new, they will take patience to work out.

Chapter *3*

How the European Community Works

T he structure of the European Community and its power to bring about change is based on the treaties of Paris and Rome and the Schuman Plan. These documents established the EC's predecessor organizations: the European Coal and Steel Community (ECSC), the European Atomic Energy Community (Euratom), and the European Economic Community (EEC).

The ECSC, Euratom, and the EEC, are now joined under the administrative system of the European Community. The EC has the authority to adopt laws regarding agriculture, industrial standards, transportation, tariffs, and other economic issues.

The EC is set up like the governments of many democratic countries, the United States included. In order to provide checks and balances it has four branches: the Commission (the executive branch), the Council of Ministers (the legislative branch), the Court of Justice (the judicial branch), and the European Parliament, which acts primarily as an advisory group.

A Supernational System

What is most extraordinary about the EC system is that it is supernational. That means its members have given up

Four main branches of government will provide the framework for daily operation

Opposite:
The Council of Ministers and the Commission will be based primarily in Brussels, Belgium. The EEC Palace (shown here) will be a central meeting place for these two branches.

part of their sovereignty (or independence) to the EC. The powers of the EC are in areas of government that cannot be handled effectively by the individual nations. Instead, they work together for the common good.

For example, the EC has taken on the task of preserving and protecting the environment—something that affects all of its citizens; and something that can be done more successfully on a large-scale level than by each individual member nation. On May 7, 1990, the decision was made to set up a European Environment Agency in order to tackle the problems of the ozone layer, wilderness protection, preservation of the rain forests, soil erosion, and other issues. The EC is also involved in unifying road, rail, and air transportation safety standards so they can be the same among all twelve nations.

In addition, supernationality means the EC can set standards on the fundamental rights of workers, including vocational training, health care, safety, and equal rights. However, like all of the other changes taking place within the EC right now, these are still in the evolutionary phase. The EC is a system in the making, a system that has yet to achieve its final goals.

Of course, the system is not without its problems. Throughout its history, the EC has experienced conflicts among its members on Community matters. Most of these conflicts occur when member nations are unwilling to put community needs ahead of their own interests. Agricultural issues have proved particularly difficult to resolve.

Nevertheless, since being formulated in the 1950s, the EC has accomplished a great deal, including a series of acts and treaties to help make "one Europe" a reality. Community nations have already experienced rapid economic growth; they have recorded large increases in per capita (per person) national income, total value of goods and services produced, and volume of trade. One of the most important acts the group has taken was to ratify the Single European Act in 1985. This act allowed more decisions to be made by majority vote of the Council of Ministers.

THE FOUR BRANCHES OF GOVERNMENT

Brussels, Belgium

The Commission: 17 members

- **Executive Branch**
- Sees that treaties and laws are carried out
- Only branch able to propose legislation
- Can take action against EC rules violations

Brussels, Belgium

The Council of Ministers: 12 members

- **Legislative Branch**
- Can accept or reject proposals
- Can request proposals from Commission

Strasbourg, France

The European Parliament: 518 members

- **Advisory Branch**
- Debates Commission's proposals
- Acts as sounding board for European opinion
- Members directly elected by member EC countries; number per country decided by population
- Can reject legislation from the Council of Ministers
- Can expel the entire Commission with a two-thirds majority vote
- Approves EC budget

Kirchberg, Luxembourg

The Court of Justice: 13 judges; 6 advocates general

- **Judicial Branch**
- Acts as the EC Supreme Court
- Determines whether acts of Commission, the Council, member governments, and private organizations are in accordance with founding treaties
- Decisions are binding on all branches and member-nation governments

The Four Branches

Each branch of the EC government will handle a specific aspect of the Community. As with the government of the United States, the powers of each branch are tempered by the powers of other branches. Briefly, here's what each branch does:

The Commission is the executive branch of the EC, the initiator and executor. It sees that the foundation treaties

Jacques Delors—
President of the European Community

The success of Western Europe's unification efforts are due in large measure to its strong-minded president, Jacques Delors. A shrewd and sometimes outspoken Frenchman, he became the EC's president in 1985. It was Delors who selected the year 1992 as the target date for eliminating trade barriers among the twelve member nations.

When he became president at the age of 65, Delors found upon his arrival in Brussels that the European Community was almost at a standstill, bogged down in bureaucracy and politics. He immediately began an intense campaign to get 1992 accepted as the final target date for eliminating trade barriers among the Community's twelve members. His enthusiasm and dedication earned him the nickname "Mr. Europe."

Delors is a self-made man, the hardworking son of a messenger for the Banque de France. After graduating from high school, he worked for his father's employer during the day and at night went to school, earning two degrees, one in law and one in economics. From 1969 to 1972, he was an adviser to France's Prime Minister Jacques Chaban-Delmas. From 1981 to 1984, he was the minister of economy and finance under France's President François Mitterrand.

With a reputation for being short-tempered and outspoken at times, Delors once referred to a British

Jacques Delors

representative on the sixteen-member European Commission as "a lackey of the Labour Party."

Delors lives with his wife, Marie, in a five-room apartment in Paris. They have a married daughter, Martine. Their only son, Jean Paul, died of cancer several years ago. Delors's hobbies and interests are jazz, movies, soccer, and the annual Tour de France bicycle race. Twice he has served as a television commentator for the Tour de France.

that created the European Community are carried out and that legislation passed by the Council is put into effect. It is the only branch allowed to propose legislation, called the "right of initiative." The Commission can take legal action against persons, companies, or member states that violate EC rules. It manages the EC budget and represents the EC in international trade negotiations. The Commission consists of seventeen commissioners who are chosen by unanimous agreement to serve four-year terms. There are two from France, Germany, Italy, Spain, and the United Kingdom; one each from the other member nations. They are appointed for four-year terms by common agreement among the member states. The president and six vice presidents are appointed from among the commissioners for two years. All terms are renewable. All commissioners must pledge to put aside their national and personal interests in favor of the common good when making decisions. The Commission has an administrative staff, based mainly in Brussels and, to a lesser extent, Luxembourg. It consists of about 14,000 officials, divided between some twenty directorates-general. Twenty-three percent of the Commission's personnel is employed on the linguistic work made necessary by the fact there are nine working languages among the EC nations.

The Council of Ministers is the EC's policy-making group. It consists of ministers from the twelve national governments. In the beginning, decisions in many areas required a unanimous vote. But many times the ministers could not agree and nothing much happened. The Single European Act changed voting policy and now many decisions can be made by a majority vote. Although the Council cannot propose legislation, it can accept or reject the Commission's proposals. It can also request that the Commission make proposals. Specialty councils meet to discuss related matters. For example, the agriculture ministers discuss farm prices. The finance ministers discuss employment and monetary matters. The presidency of the Council is held for a six-month term in the following order: Belgium, Denmark, Germany, Greece, Spain, France, Ireland, Italy, Luxembourg, Netherlands, Portugal, and the UK. The Council meets primarily in Brussels.

The European Parliament is an advisory board. Think of it as the voice of democracy, the melting pot of all twelve nations. Its main purpose is to debate the Commission's proposals. The best way to understand its exact function is to envision it as a sounding board for European opinion. It may also request changes or modifications on issues. Its 518 members are directly elected in each of the member countries. The exact number of members of Parliament that can be elected by each country is in proportion to its population. Currently, the countries with the largest representation are Germany, Great Britain, France, and Italy. Members are elected for a five-year term and represent a broad spectrum of the political parties that are active in Europe. Although the Parliament's role is primarily advisory, it has certain rights and powers. The Single European Act of 1985 gave it increased powers through a procedure called "concertation," in which it can reject certain legislation from the Council. It also can expel the entire Commission if two-thirds of its members vote to do so. So far, it has not used this dramatic power. The European Parliament meets in Strasbourg, France, although its administrative staff, called the Secretariat, meets in Luxembourg.

The Court of Justice is the EC's supreme court. It consists of thirteen judges plus six advocates-general who assist them. Terms for both groups last six years. The Court determines whether the actions of the Commission, the Council, member governments, and even private organizations are operating in accordance with the founding treaties. Private citizens, member countries, the Commission, and the Council can also ask the Court to hear appeals. Any decision the Court of Justice makes is binding on everyone involved, including the member governments. The Court meets in Luxembourg at Palais de la Cour de Justice, Kirchberg, Luxembourg.

The Parliament building in Strasbourg, France, will be home to the EC's 518 parliamentary members.

Behind the Scenes

The EC is growing even as you read this book. And there is still much work to be done. Translators (to help the twelve nations communicate), secretaries, and others, are constantly added to the roster of EC workers. Presently, there are approximately 25,000 people worldwide working for the EC.

Various organizations and committees do much of the administrative day-to-day work of the EC. The General

Secretariat, which has about 2,000 employees, is based primarily in Brussels. The administrative staff of the Commission totals about 14,000 people.

Funding

At one time the European Community received its operating money from member contributions. Today, however, it has its own healthy resources. It collects customs and

A Conflict with Great Britain

The Court of Justice

In the middle of October 1991, the European Community threatened to take legal action to stop seven major British construction projects, including the high-speed rail link between London and the new English Channel tunnel. What was behind the threat? Primarily, opposing nations had environmental concerns. The European Commission said the British projects were not developed according to the EC's environmental regulations and it might seek a court order to halt construction. If necessary, the Commission will ask the European Community's Court of Justice to give a final opinion on whether the projects are really a threat to the environment.

The British viewed the move as high-handed and unnecessary on the part of the EC. Great Britain had been leery of letting go of its authority in order to create a larger European political union. William Cash, a Conservative leader in the British House of Commons, summed up the British position about the EC. "They are trying to push Britain into a corner and we won't be pushed."

The British planned to run part of the Channel rail link through sparsely populated areas that include marshlands. The EC said this would be environmentally dangerous. Other British projects under EC attack include a bridge that will cut through and eight-thousand-year-old forest in Greenwich, southeast of London; a soft-drink factory; a hospital incinerator; and a refinery.

Britain was given two months to respond to the charges or face defending its position in the Community's Court of Justice. If the conflict persists, use of the Court of Justice would be the first major test of the EC's judicial system.

THE EC BUDGET

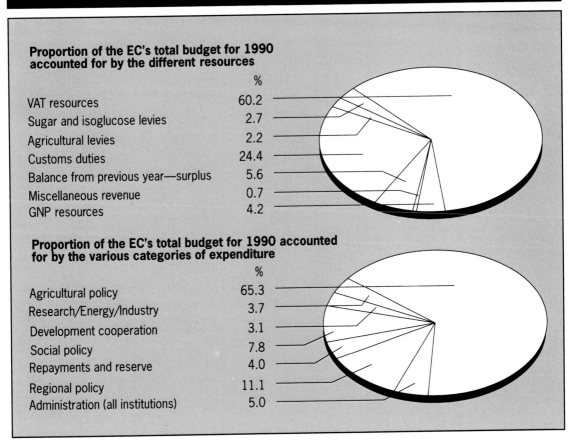

**Proportion of the EC's total budget for 1990
accounted for by the different resources**

	%
VAT resources	60.2
Sugar and isoglucose levies	2.7
Agricultural levies	2.2
Customs duties	24.4
Balance from previous year—surplus	5.6
Miscellaneous revenue	0.7
GNP resources	4.2

**Proportion of the EC's total budget for 1990 accounted
for by the various categories of expenditure**

	%
Agricultural policy	65.3
Research/Energy/Industry	3.7
Development cooperation	3.1
Social policy	7.8
Repayments and reserve	4.0
Regional policy	11.1
Administration (all institutions)	5.0

agricultural duties on imports from the world outside the
EC. It also assesses a proportion of sales tax (VAT, for
Value-Added Tax) collected in member countries. In
addition, it is entitled to funds from each country based on
that country's gross national product.

The EC's budget is supervised by the Court of Auditors.
There are twelve auditors, and they serve for six-year terms.
This court examines the EC's expenditures and receipts.

The EC also has access to some funds from the European Investment Bank. This bank, established by the
Treaty of Rome, is an independent institution within the
EC. It makes loans to member states and raises funds for
the ECSC and Euratom.

The EC and the USA: Distant Cousins?

There are many similarities between the formation and structure of the European Community and that of America. If we look at our own history, we see that the European Community and America have shared many common circumstances. Consider the following:

The original thirteen colonies in our country abolished all internal tariffs when forming the new United States.

The EC wants to create a unified trading marketplace, one without internal tariffs.

Many of the original thirteen colonies had their own currency and monetary systems. Today, the United States has a single currency.

The European Community wants to have a single currency rather than twelve different ones. After 1992, each member country will accept the currency of other member nations.

America's founders worried about turning over too much power to a central authority and were suspicious of too strong a central government. To combat this fear, the United States divided governmental power into three branches: the executive, the legislative, and the judicial.

The EC, also fearful of a strong central power, has divided its balance of power among four branches: the executive (the Commission), the legislative (the Council of Ministers), the advisory (the European Parliament), and the judicial (the Court of Justice).

Americans, though patriotic, proudly cling to their regional and state identities with great loyalty. Even though Americans have regional differences, they are unified by a common federal law and national heritage. Each state has its own unique flag, for example, but all state flags fly below the common flag of the United States.

Europeans are eager to enjoy the benefits of a unified common market yet, at the same time, are suspicious of losing their national identities. In the coming years, member countries will struggle to find a balance between individual identity and membership to a greater union.

United States Support

The European Community and the United States share, among many things, a commitment to democracy. In fact, the United States played a major role in beginning the European unification in 1947, when Secretary of State George Marshall launched the European Recovery Program. Popularly known as the "Marshall Plan," it made huge amounts of financial aid available from the United States for the reconstruction of a Europe devastated by World War II. There was one condition for receiving this aid, however: The countries had to agree to administer the U.S. aid jointly. This need for cooperation between countries helped to create the first post-war common European organization—the Organization for European Economic Cooperation (OEEC).

Since the beginning of the European Community, the officials of the EC and the United States have exchanged many ideas. U.S. cabinet members and EC commissioners have maintained close contact through the Commission's delegation in Washington, D.C., and the U.S. Mission to the European Communities. Starting in the early 1980s, the U.S. secretary of state and the EC Commission president have met each year in Brussels. Both organizations enjoy diplomatic status and work together communicating the viewpoint of the U.S. government to the EC.

What the EC Means for the United States

As 1992 unfolds, so should opportunities for U.S. companies, especially those that do a great deal of business outside America. No longer will American firms need to work from separate bases within each European country or pay the costs of meeting dozens of different local rules and regulations. During the past, their competitors focused on the well-protected home markets while the U.S. corporations built plants and facilities in Europe. These American companies are ready and able to expand in 1992.

Small and midsized American companies that export to the EC will have new opportunities. They will be selling into a single market that basically has uniform standards, norms, testing, and certification procedures. In other words, the manufacturer of a certain product or implement will no longer

face twelve different sets of national requirements, import rules, and border controls.

As the economies of the twelve member nations improve and grow, there should also be more demand for U.S. goods and services. In fact, business between the U.S. and the EC is already booming. The EC is currently the largest market for American products. It buys one fourth of American exports and accounts for two fifths of American external direct investment.

For American exporters, bureaucratic costs and delays have already melted away with the use of the Single Administrative Document. In the past, American companies estimated that the documentation process alone added between three and five percent to the total cost of goods sold in European countries. Customs delays generally doubled distribution time. And national rules prevented truckers from returning with a loaded truck after delivery across a border.

By using one European country as a homebase, a company can do business throughout the entire EC market. According to a 1990 survey of over nine hundred U.S. and European business executives, conducted by Louis Harris and Associates, one third of U.S. businesses already have facilities in Europe. Another eight percent expect to be there within the next five years. Manufacturers stand to gain enormously once transportation is deregulated and taxes are standardized.

Indeed, many American companies established in Europe are likely to be treated as domestic companies once the single market becomes a reality. IBM, AT&T, Ford, and Philip Morris have long done business in Europe and have much to gain by unification. So, too, do companies with products we all recognize, such as Kraft and General Foods. They have been selling goods to Europe for many years.

Experts predict a unified Germany will eventually be an economic powerhouse because it will be the gateway to trade with the emerging democracies of the Eastern European countries.

The opportunity exists, therefore, for American firms with a presence in Europe to jump on the bandwagon. They have much to gain from both the unified European market and the establishment of open markets throughout Eastern Europe.

Chapter 4

Europe Without Barriers: 1992 and Beyond

The year 1992 was chosen more for symbolic value than practical application. By designating a specific year in which to declare the EC "officially united," the twelve members are solidifying future plans and celebrating their accomplishments to date. But the end of 1992 will not bring any magical results, no dramatic changes in the look or functioning of the day-to-day in Europe. It will simply signal the beginning of a new era; one in which there is much work yet to be done.

> The EC has chosen 1992 as the symbolic year to signal the beginning of a new era

In the Works: The Three Hundred Proposals

Initially, the EC had three hundred specific proposals (in what was called the White Paper) for unifying the twelve member states by 1992. The number was later trimmed to 279. So far, almost two hundred are on their way to becoming law or have been adopted; the rest are still being debated or revised. The proposals make it possible for investments and money to move freely across borders, for customs formalities between countries to end by 1993, and to start a European Central Bank by 1999.

Of course, some things still have to be ironed out. Take, for example, food crossing the border lines. What if an English citizen buys pasta from Italy? Will the label be in

Opposite:
In the Europe of the future, citizens from all nations will travel easily from country to country and will be able to share their cultures more freely.

Italian? Will a Spaniard be able to read the label on canned vegetables coming from France? In all likelihood, most products—across the board—will be labeled in French and English. But certain products that are *only* going to Spain, for example, may just be labeled in Spanish. It depends on the product's ultimate destination.

The European Standard of Living

What will European life be like after 1992? In all probability, changes will be slow in coming. As with anything new, there needs to be a transitional period. New questions will be raised and new rules will have to be made. In the interim, there will be many painful decisions and compromises that have to be worked out.

Generally, the people of Europe look forward to the EC changes with a mixture of excitement, fear, and some skepticism. Many hope the unification will make their lives easier and more comfortable. But many also worry about the effect the new structure will have on their jobs and the ability of their country's industries to compete globally with other major industrial nations.

For the most part, however, Europeans should be optimistic. From what you've read so far, it's easy to understand how the new laws will translate into economic and political success on a large scale. This is what individual citizens in EC member nations can expect:

Moving People
1) There will be no passport checks at borders within the EC for EC members. Eventually, there may even be one passport for all Europeans.

2) Tourists from other nations, such as the United States, will also be able to move from nation to nation within the EC without constant passport checks. Presently, visitors going from New York to London to Rome, for example, have to go through customs twice: once in London and again in Rome. After 1992, travelers will go

through customs only once—at their point of entry in Europe—and will not have to check in again, regardless of where else in Europe they travel.

3) Due to the benefits created by the EC, the number of people traveling throughout Europe will increase. Europeans will travel to member countries for school and work more often than in the past. Visas will no longer be necessary both for tourists and other travelers.

4) Universities will be open to students from any member country. University degrees and diplomas will be recognized throughout the EC.

5) The Erasmus Program (European Community Action Scheme for the Mobility of Students) will make it possible for a student to transfer easily from one EC university to a university in another EC country.

6) The development of a common language is still seen as very remote. But the Lingua Program (Community Action Program to Promote Foreign Language Competence in the European Community) will encourage student exchanges in secondary and higher education for foreign languages. Students, however, already learn at least three languages in school; and English is the universal language.

With an overall higher standard of living for its people, a united Europe expects a stimulated economy and a stronger environment for commerce and investment. Here, shoppers in Berlin flock to Woolworth's as the store opens its doors.

7) People will be able to work in the member country of their choice. Professionals in fields such as medicine, dentistry, law, architecture, and accountancy will be able to work anywhere within the twelve countries. Nonprofessionals will also be able to work in any of the EC countries on the same terms, and with the same chances of success as nationals of the host country.

8) Workers across all EC countries will be entitled to certain overall benefits, including health care, retirement, equal rights, and so on.

Moving Goods

1) Goods will move freely within the EC, without tariffs or restrictions. Goods will no longer be delayed at the borders. Goods will also be subject to uniform safety measures, environmental and consumer protection standards. Food labeling, in particular, will likely be standardized in French and English. (No room for twelve languages on a cereal box!) And the consumer in each member state will be able to choose the product he or she prefers: pasta made from durum wheat, or beer made from entirely natural ingredients.

2) Producers and manufacturers will have a huge market to sell to—about 340 million consumers. Consumers will benefit, too, because they will have a wider choice of goods and services, at more competitive prices.

A Free Exchange of Services

1) Individuals with services to perform will move as freely as goods.

2) Travel will be less expensive as airlines and railroad systems compete for passengers. Safety standards will be mutually agreed upon.

3) Currently, the EC has fewer telephones and television sets than North American countries, but that will improve as networks are modernized, more satellites are installed, and service is standardized. There will be more programs

A New Europe for the Young

Getting to know their European neighbors and to live among them has always been a popular experience for Europe's young people. The EC recognizes the value of this interaction and is working to make it easier for young people, workers, students, teachers, and scientists to move more freely between their lands. Plans for the future include:

Youth for Europe, which promotes an increase in exchanges for young people in the fifteen to twenty-five age group.

The European young workers' exchange program aims to offer training or work experience in another member state to young people between ages eighteen and twenty-eight. The program was recently opened up to include those looking for jobs.

The *Erasmus Program* hopes to increase the free movement of students, thus improving their understanding of fellow Europeans. It covers various activities: an inter-university cooperation system, measures to extend academic recognition of diplomas, and grants to enable students in higher education to spend a period of training in another member state.

Students relax together in Segovia, Spain.

Comett is developing partnerships between universities and firms to continue the training of students looking for jobs in new scientific technologies.

Vocational training and research is the goal of *Petra,* which, like the others, promotes transnational partnerships, initiatives, and projects managed by the young people themselves.

Lingua aims to improve citizens' language skills by promoting student exchanges in secondary and higher education, teacher training, and so on.

and television channels for all. For example, Britons will be able to choose between Danish programs, German programs, Greek programs, and so on. Telephone service between the member nations will also be improved. A tangled web of mobile telephone services has already been replaced with a single Europe-wide system.

Moving Capital

1) Citizens will be able to travel throughout the EC using the currency of their choice.

2) Everyone will be free to save money or invest wherever he or she likes within the EC. It will be easy to buy stocks and bonds in any of the twelve countries.

3) People will be able to choose among many investments offered by member countries, such as mortgages, bank savings plans, and insurance.

The EC as a Political Force

In November 1991, the EC decided to impose economic sanctions on Yugoslavia. The sanctions were designed to pressure the Yugoslavian government to end a civil war between Serbs and Croats. At a meeting in Rome on November 8, 1991, the Community voted to withdraw trade preferences from Yugoslavia, to terminate an agreement for economic aid, and to urge the United Nations to impose an oil embargo against the country.

The EC's actions were an important step in gaining political respect for the Community. Acting as one political unit, the twelve nations exerted considerable pressure on another nation. They showed the world, in real terms, just how powerful the EC can be. For Yugoslavia, the EC's power was all too real; sixty percent of Yugoslavia's trade is with the Community.

Can Europe Truly Unite?

Fantasies and wild ideas do some true. After years of discussion, Paris and London will soon be connected when the Chunnel—the tunnel under the English Channel—is completed.

Polls show that a majority of the citizens of the EC countries support further integration. In 1989, a European Commission survey showed that five out of eight favored creating a European union. In the "Euro-barometer" survey conducted for the EC Commission in

Who Wants to Join

Initially, a group of countries, known as the Outer Seven, did not join the EC. They were the United Kingdom, Norway, Sweden, Denmark, Austria, Portugal, and Switzerland. They didn't want to give up their independence; they didn't like the terms they'd have to agree to, and they didn't see the overall benefits. Three of these nations have since joined: the U.K., Denmark, and Portugal.

Countries that now want to join include Sweden (applied for membership 1989); Austria (applied for membership 1991); Turkey (applied for membership 1987); and Malta and Cyprus (applied for membership 1990).

The EC would like to expand beyond its twelve members but is wary about whom to let in. Article 237 of the Rome treaty states: "any European state may apply to become a member of the Community." This general invitation, however, has restrictions. Basically, only those countries with a *democratic* form of government are eligible to join. The main requirement for joining is political stability, and, at the moment, many East European countries that would like to join do not yet qualify. The countries most likely to get in the soonest include Austria and Sweden.

However, it is unlikely any new members will be admitted until *after* 1992. The EC has too many other issues at the moment and would ideally like to sort out its new menu for economic and political union before it lets anyone else in. The EC "club" will probably not admit anyone else until the mid-1990s. The EC in the year 2000 will most likely be quite different from the EC that exists today. William Wallace, deputy director of the Royal Institute of International Affairs, and author of a new study, "The Transformation of Western Europe," predicts a Community of twenty or more nations, with a total population of over 400 million.

The membership process is a list of complicated political criteria. There is still a lot of animosity, rivalry, and competition between some countries. Now that all twelve nations have to agree, the process of admitting new members will be long and difficult.

Like so many issues presently on the EC's docket, there is division between the twelve members over whom to admit. Prime Minister John Major of Britain argues that the Community should welcome Eastern and Central European countries "as soon as they are ready politically and economically." He has said, "We must be prepared to widen our horizons and widen our membership." Yet President François Mitterand of France recently warned that Eastern Europe might still be decades away from full Community membership.

The Community has already begun implementing policies to give short-term and medium-term support to the reform process of Eastern Europe and the Soviet Union. It has taken immediate actions to grant these countries better access to its markets, to provide financial aid, to offer technical assistance and training, to facilitate foreign investment, and to help clean up the entire continent's environment.

NATIONS THAT WANT TO JOIN
- Have applied for membership
- Undecided
- Possible future application

A British worker and French worker celebrate the first connection between England and France in the Chunnel, 1990.

late 1988, more than half the populations of EC member states said they favored the efforts made to unify Western Europe. (The Danes and the British were the least positive overall.)

A totally united Europe is still a somewhat distant goal. There is much to be done before December 31, 1992. Yet despite the diversity of member countries, much has already been accomplished toward real and lasting unity. As the advantages of union become more obvious, and the shock of change fades into the background, a truly united Europe will indeed become less a dream and more a reality.

EUROSPEAK: A Glossary of Terms

- **Accession** To increase by addition. The act of coming together or attaining power.
- **Bretton Woods** The agreement that shaped international monetary system for twenty-five years after World War II. In 1944, officials from forty-five non-Communist countries met at Bretton Woods, New Hampshire, and agreed on an international monetary system. Exchange rates between countries were fixed in gold or the dollar. This fixed exchange rate system was in effect until the early 1970s when a floating exchange rate replaced it.
- **Capital** The word economists use for money or wealth; often used to describe the amount of money used to run a business.
- **Currency** Dollars, pounds, Deutschmarks, lira . . . in other words, money.
- **Duty** A tax based on the declared value of imported or exported goods.
- **Exchange rate** Price at which one currency can be converted into another; British pounds for Italian lira, for example.
- **Gross National Product** Total value of a country's annual output of goods and services.
- **Inflation** A rise in consumer prices (or other prices) expressed as an annual rate.
- **Nationalism** Devotion to the interests of one's own nation.
- **Protectionism** A general term for obstacles to international trade. Examples of protectionism are tariffs and quotas.
- **Quotas** A form of trade protectionism in which a country will import only so much of an item from another country during the year. Unlike tariffs, which raise the price of imports by taxing them, quotas do not provide any direct revenue for the government.
- **Recession** A period of slow, or no, economic growth.
- **Sovereignty** A territory existing as an independent state; complete independence and self-government.
- **Supernational** Greater than a nation.
- **Tariff** A schedule of duties or taxes, imposed on imports to raise money (known as a revenue tariff) or to protect domestic firms from import competition (known as a protective tariff).
- **Value added tax (VAT)** An indirect form of taxation in which the tax is levied on the value added at each stage of production. The tax is added to the cost of the item at each stage, so the total tax is paid by the final consumer.

Chronology

1949	The Council of Europe formed to join its ten member nations culturally, socially, and economically.
1950	French Foreign Minister Robert Schuman makes a proposal to place Europe's coal and steel industries under a common European authority.
1951	The Treaty of Paris signed, creating the European Coal and Steel Community (ECSC) to unify the coal, iron, and steel industries of Belgium, France, Italy, Luxembourg, the Netherlands, and West Germany.
1957	The Treaties of Rome establish the European Economic Community (EEC) and the European Atomic Energy Community (Euratom) to work on developing peaceful uses of nuclear energy.
1967	The ECSC, the EEC, and Euratom merge their agencies to form a unified administrative system.

1973 The European Community admits Great Britain, Denmark, and Ireland.

1975 All European nations (except Albania and Andorra) and Canada, Cyprus, and the U.S., meet in Helsinki, Finland, for the Conference on Security and Cooperation in Europe. They sign the first of the Helsinki Accords, pledging to work toward more cooperation in human rights, peace, and economic matters.

1979 European Monetary System (EMS) becomes operative. The citizens of the nine member states vote for the first directly elected members of the European Parliament.

1981 Greece joins the European Community.

1985 EC Heads of State and Governments endorse a "White Paper" outlining a strategy for creating a true common market by 1992. Single European Act is passed.

1986 Spain and Portugal join the European Community.

1987 The European Community acts upon the Single European Act, which establishes the end of 1992 as a deadline for ending all nontariff barriers among community members.

1989 The Heads of State and Governments meeting in Madrid endorses a plan for economic and monetary union. In December, a new political partnership between the EC and the U.S. is outlined by U.S. Secretary of State, James Baker.

1990 East and West Germany merge as united Germany. The EC Heads of State and Governments meeting in Dublin warmly welcomes German unification, reconfirms their commitment to economic and monetary union and endorses the strengthening of the EC. In November, a Transatlantic Declaration lays down the principles for EC–U.S. consultation and cooperation.

1991 Members debate future membership for Eastern European nations. EC leaders meet in December to discuss greater political union and the plan for common currency.

For Further Reading

For pamphlets and brochures:

- **The U.S. Chamber of Commerce**. International Division, 1615 H Street, NW, Washington, DC 20062; (202) 463-5460

- **Commission of the European Communities.** 2100 M Street, NW, Suite 707, Washington, DC 20037; (202) 862-9500

- **Commission of the European Communities.** 305 East 47th Street; 1 Dag Hammarskjold Plaza, New York, NY 10017; (212) 371-3804

Index

Acknowledgments and photo credits

Cover: ©Craig/SABA; p. 4: ©Anticoli-Nicozzi-Nusca/Gamma-Liaison; p. 9: ©North Wind Picture Archives; pp.10, 11, 12, 13, 14, 15, 16, 31: Wide World Photos; p. 17: UPI/Bettmann; p. 18: ©Versele/Gamma-Liaison; p. 22: ©Sahm Doherty/Gamma-Liaison; p. 24: ©George Merillon/Gamma-Liaison; pp. 25, 55: ©Eric Bouvet/Gamma-Liaison; p. 26: ©Christian Vioujard/Gamma-Liaison; p. 28: ©Eric Brissaud/ Gamma-Liaison; p. 32: ©Alexis Duclos/Gamma-Liaison; p. 36: ©Joe Traver/Gamma-Liaison; p. 38: ©Alin Buu/Gamma-Liaison; p. 40: ©Giry/SABA; p. 44: ©Ribolowski/Gamma-Liaison; p. 47: ©Damoret/ SABA; p. 48: ©Bazin-Scorceletti/Gamma-Liaison; p. 52: Gamma-Liaison; p. 57: ©Peter Menzel/Stock, Boston; p. 60: ©Decoux/SABA.

Illustration on page 51 by Wendy F. Axel.
Maps and charts by David Bell.

Special thanks to Cindy Dopkin and Elvis Brathwaite.